8/18

The Milky Way

by Grace Hansen

Abdo
OUR GALAXY
Kids

abdopublishing.com

Published by Abdo Kids, a division of ABDO, P.O. Box 398166, Minneapolis, Minnesota 55439.

Printed in the United States of America, North Mankato, Minnesota.

052017

092017

THIS BOOK CONTAINS
RECYCLED MATERIALS

Photo Credits: iStock, ESO, NASA, Shutterstock

Production Contributors: Teddy Borth, Jennie Forsberg, Grace Hansen

Design Contributors: Dorothy Toth, Laura Mitchell

Publisher's Cataloging in Publication Data

Names: Hansen, Grace, author.

Title: The Milky Way / by Grace Hansen.

Description: Minneapolis, Minnesota : Abdo Kids, 2018 | Series: Our galaxy |
    Includes bibliographical references and index.

Identifiers: LCCN 2016962404 | ISBN 9781532100529 (lib. bdg.) |
    ISBN 9781532101212 (ebook) | ISBN 9781532101762 (Read-to-me ebook)

Subjects: LCSH: Milky Way--Juvenile literature.

Classification: DDC 523.1/13--dc23

LC record available at http://lccn.loc.gov/2016962404

Table of Contents

How the Milky Way Was Made

The Milky Way is a galaxy.

Our **solar system** is in the

Milky Way. There are also

billions of stars and much more!

5

The universe is around
13.82 billion years old.
The young universe was
very hot and **dense**. No
gases could form.

As time went on, the universe cooled and spread out. It was still very hot. But it had cooled enough that **hydrogen**, **helium**, and other gases could form.

The gases formed large clouds. The universe continued to cool and expand. **Gravity** took over and caused the clouds to **collapse**. This formed massive stars.

11

Later, the stars exploded!
The heat from this caused
larger gas clouds to **collapse**.
Finally, the clouds and stars
came together to form galaxies.

13

A Spiral Galaxy

The Milky Way is a barred spiral galaxy. It is a large, flat spinning disc. It is made up of gas, dust, and stars. There is a bulge in the center. It is made up of old red stars.

15

Spiraling outward from the disc are four main arms. The arms contain most of the galaxy's gas and dust. Many young stars are in the arms!

our solar system

17

The Center of Our Galaxy

A halo surrounds the Milky Way.

It is made up partly of old stars.

At the center of the galaxy is a

supermassive **black hole**.

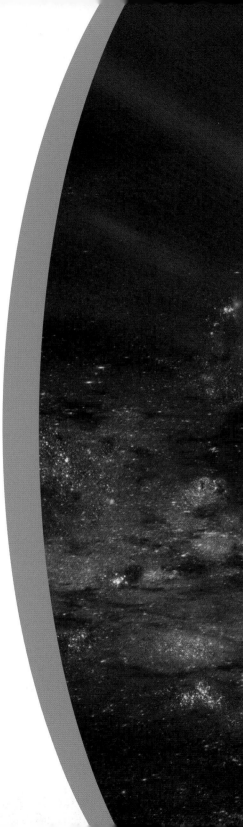

19

The **black hole** formed at the same time the Milky Way did. It has four million times the mass of our Sun. It has so much **gravity** that our entire galaxy **orbits** it.

21

More Facts

- The supermassive **black hole** at the center of the Milky Way is called Sagittarius A*.

- Scientists believe that in about 5 billion years, the Milky Way will collide with the Andromeda Galaxy.

- The Milky Way is just one of billions of galaxies in the universe.

Glossary

black hole – an invisible place in space where gravity pulls so much that even light cannot escape. More than 1 million suns can fit inside a supermassive black hole.

collapse – cave in.

dense – packed close together.

gravity – the force by which all objects in the universe are attracted to each other.

helium – a light, colorless gas that does not burn.

hydrogen – a gas that is lighter than air and catches fire easily.

orbit – the curved path of a planet, moon, or other object around a larger celestial body.

solar system – a group of planets and other celestial bodies that are held by the sun's gravity and revolve around it.

Index

abdokids.com

Use this code to log on to abdokids.com and access crafts, games, videos and more!

Abdo Kids Code:
OTK0529